W9-DIO-152

SOCCER CRAZY!

THIS IS A CARLTON BOOK

Text, design and illustration © Carlton Books Limited 2016

Authors: Simon Mugford, Iain Spragg and Adrian Clarke
Editor: Russell McLean
Design: ROCKJAW Creative
Design manager: Emily Clarke
Picture research: Steve Behan
Production: Charlotte Larcombe

Published in 2016 by Carlton Books Limited,
an imprint of the Carlton Publishing Group,
20 Mortimer Street, London, W1T 3JW

All rights reserved. This book is sold subject to the condition that it may not be reproduced, stored in a retrieval system or transmitted in any form or by any means, electronic, mechanical, photocopying, recording, or otherwise, without the publisher's prior consent.

A catalogue record for this book is available from the British Library.

ISBN: 978-1-78312-241-7

Printed in China

SOCCER CRAZY!

CARLTON KiDS

CONTENTS

Note to readers: all facts and figures are accurate as of 1 May 2016.

CHAPTER 1
THE JOY OF FOOTBALL

ROBERT'S RECORDS

When Wolfsburg went in at half-time 1-0 up against Bayern Munich in September 2015, they were half way to a fifth clean sheet in a row – but Bayern's Robert Lewandowski had other ideas... Coming on as a sub, he scored an incredible five goals in just nine minutes. The Polish sensation set a record for the quickest Bundesliga hat-trick in history, then set a new record for the fastest four-goal haul in one Bundesliga match, and yet another record with his fifth strike!

The 90 minutes of a football match can bring nail-biting drama, wonder goals and amazing saves – but things don't always go to plan! Read on to meet the game's greatest jokers, giggle at some goalkeeper gaffes and despair at defenders' back-pass disasters.

WONDER GOALS

Goals come in all shapes and styles, but every fan dreams of seeing the wonder strike – the dazzling goal that takes your breath away. These examples show that on some occasions, dreams really do come true!

Brilliant Brazil

Brazil's 1970 World Cup side were one of the best ever international teams and their fourth goal in the final against Italy proved it. Pelé calmly laid the ball off for Carlos Alberto, who was steaming down the right. Alberto shot while he was still running and scored what became known as the 'perfect goal'.

WONDER WAYNE

Wayne Rooney's sensational bicycle kick against Manchester City in 2011 was voted the greatest goal of the Premier League's first 20 years. After scoring only four league goals in seven months, the Manchester United forward's incredible overhead strike proved he could still deliver when it mattered.

Wayne gears up to let fly his sensational bicycle kick.

TAKE ZLAT!

When Sweden lined up against England in 2012 for what could have been another uneventful friendly, it was anything but. Of the six goals scored, four came from Sweden's pony-tailed talisman Zlatan Ibrahimović. Not content with a hat-trick, Zlatan responded to England keeper Joe Hart's headed clearance with a stunning overhead kick from 25 metres out. Even the England fans stood and applauded his super strike!

Always modest, Zlatan once said, "I can't help but laugh at how perfect I am."

Balotelli scored both of Italy's goals, then dedicated them to his mum. Bless!

Mario's rocket

When Italy beat Germany in the EURO 2012 semi-final, Italy's Mario Balotelli produced a wonder goal almost from nowhere. There seemed little danger from Riccardo Montolivo's hopeful long pass forwards, but Balotelli burst clear of the German defence and unleashed a sizzling shot from 18 metres out and into the roof of the net.

HOW DID THEY MISS THAT?

Most footballers dream of putting the ball in the back of the net. But that dream can turn into a nightmare when, with the goal firmly in their sights, panic sets in and – whoops – they send the ball in completely the wrong direction.

Villa double miss

Spanish striker David Villa wasn't on form when Spain played Colombia just a few months after being crowned world champions in 2010. With the goal there for the taking, Villa not only hit the post, but slammed the rebound so wide that the ball actually went out for a throw-in! He did make up for his double howler, however, by finding the back of the net five minutes from time.

IWELUMO INCIDENT

Scotland striker Chris Iwelumo was left scratching his head in disbelief when he failed to score against Norway in 2008. Gary Naismith saw Iwelumo meet his perfect cross just a metre in front of goal, only for his team-mate to side-foot the ball back towards him rather than past the stranded Norwegian keeper. A classic open-goal miss!

To make matters worse for Iwelumo, this match was his international debut!

Torres' disappointment continued all season at Chelsea – he scored only 11 goals in 49 games.

Torres torture

Spanish striker Fernando Torres didn't exactly live up to his £50-million price tag when playing for Chelsea against Manchester United in 2011. He scored in the game at Old Trafford but made the headlines for all the wrong reasons when he took the ball past United goalkeeper David de Gea but then stuck out an awkward left foot and stabbed his shot wide of the post. Doh!

Cristiano crisis

Even the world's greatest players can have an unexplained horror show in front of goal. Cristiano Ronaldo did just that for Manchester United against Sheffield United in 2006. Ryan Giggs split the Sheffield defence apart with a dazzling dribble and passed to an unmarked Ronaldo, only for the Portuguese star to casually chip the ball harmlessly over the crossbar.

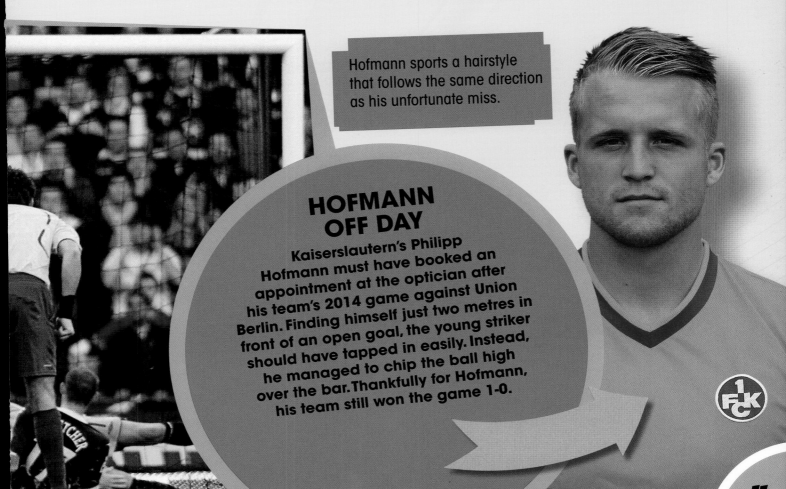

Hofmann sports a hairstyle that follows the same direction as his unfortunate miss.

HOFMANN OFF DAY

Kaiserslautern's Philipp Hofmann must have booked an appointment at the optician after his team's 2014 game against Union Berlin. Finding himself just two metres in front of an open goal, the young striker should have tapped in easily. Instead, he managed to chip the ball high over the bar. Thankfully for Hofmann, his team still won the game 1-0.

BACK-PASS DISASTERS

Football should really be played going forwards. After all, the idea is to break down the opposition defence and score goals. Sometimes, a player forgets this and goes in the other direction, passing the ball back to his goalkeeper. Quite often, this is just asking for trouble…

Dixon disaster

Arsenal and England defender Lee Dixon made an incredible mistake in 1991 when Arsenal faced Coventry. The full-back got the ball 30 metres from his own goal but with no options ahead of him, he decided to knock it back to goalkeeper David Seaman. Unfortunately Dixon didn't check where Seaman was and skilfully chipped his own keeper with a brilliant but disastrous back pass.

FABIEN FAIL

Back passes are only as good as the goalkeeper on the receiving end of them. A lapse in concentration can turn a perfectly good ball into a disaster. A classic example came in 2001 when Manchester United's Fabien Barthez got a beautiful back pass from David Beckham. Under absolutely no pressure, Barthez hit his clearance straight to Arsenal's Thierry Henry on the edge of the box, who couldn't believe his luck and scored.

Barthez followed this up five minutes later by dropping the ball and letting Henry score again!

Paul Robinson stares at the pitch as he considers a future career as a groundsman.

Inigo in

Spanish footballers are famous for their silky skills, but defender Inigo Martinez lacked them while on Under-21 duty for his country in 2011 against Georgia. The Georgian keeper launched a hopeful long-range kick up the field, but for some reason Martinez decided to volley the ball back to his keeper with an eye-catching back heel. Unfortunately, his effort ballooned off his boot, over his irate goalie and into the net from 40 metres out.

DIVOT DANGER

Bumpy pitches are a nightmare for players at all levels of the beautiful game and even top-class internationals are wary of the dangers of an uneven surface. Just ask England goalkeeper Paul Robinson, who had to pick the ball out of his own net in a EURO 2008 qualifier against Croatia in Zagreb after Gary Neville's back pass hit a divot and bobbled over his swinging right boot.

CELEBRATING IN STYLE

In the old days, goals would be celebrated with a simple handshake, but those times are long since over. Today, it's all about outrageous back flips, dynamic dance moves or even the use of random comedy props! Here are some players who go over the top when they hit the back of the net.

MOCK THE MANAGER

Curly-haired prankster Jimmy Bullard cheekily poked fun at his Hull City manager Phil Brown in 2009 by re-enacting the half-time team talk Brown had given them on the pitch at Manchester City's stadium the previous season. After scoring a penalty, the midfielder gathered his team-mates in a circle in the same spot and pretended to give them a talking to! Even Brown himself was in stitches on the sidelines.

Phil Brown said of Jimmy Bullard's prank, "Great comedy is all about timing."

Lots of players take off their shirts to celebrate a goal, but Montenegro star Mirko Vučinić went further in 2010 after finding the back of the net against Switzerland. He took off his shorts, stuck them onto his head and ran around in his underwear like a man who had, er, lost his trousers. Vučinić repeated the celebration in Serie A for Juventus.

Klinsmann demonstrates his amazing skills of levitation on the pitch.

Diving down

German striker Jürgen Klinsmann was often criticised for going down too easily under challenges during his spells with Tottenham Hotspur in the 1990s. His response was to perform a spectacular 'splash dive' when he scored! His team-mates loved it too and half the team hit the deck chest first each time Klinsmann found the back of the net.

CENSORED!

Fishing fun

If trophies were awarded for clever goal celebrations, Icelandic side Stjarnan would win the Champions League. Their players gained fame with routines such as the Human Bicycle, Rambo and Giving Birth. The best came in 2010 after a goal against Fylkir, when striker Halldor Orri caught Jóhann 'The Salmon' Laxdaal on his imaginary fishing line and reeled him in, much to the amusement of millions of viewers on the internet. Jóhann's realistic portrayal of the panic-stricken, bouncing salmon was truly a sight to behold.

Carrot top

What do you do when you want to taunt your opponents who are nicknamed the Rabbits? According to Atletico Mineiro's Brazilian forward Edmilson Ferreira, it's easy. You score a goal, pull a concealed carrot out of your shorts and start eating it like a bunny.

Let's hope Mirko's mum remembered to give him a clean pair of pants.

AMAZING SAVES

The life of the goalkeeper is not always a happy one. Every mistake and lapse in concentration is analysed and criticised in minute detail. But that's all forgotten in those rare moments when the player between the sticks pulls off a truly spectacular save.

Hart racing

It's always great to see a goalkeeper go forwards to try and score from a last-minute corner, but it's often funny watching him race back to his goal in a desperate bid to stop a breakaway ball at the other end. Manchester City's Joe Hart did just this in 2010, when he was caught at the wrong end of the pitch but somehow managed to get back and punch away Wayne Rooney's brilliant 50-metre drive. City still lost 1–0 but Hart at least had won his own personal duel with Rooney.

"Do you want me to make the goal bigger for you?" laughed Schmeichel.

DANISH DEFENCE

Peter Schmeichel used to terrify opposition strikers and his own defence in equal measure as he barked out orders during his Manchester United days. The great Dane certainly had something to shout about in 1997, when he pulled off possibly the greatest save of his career to deny Newcastle's John Barnes, leaping like Superman across the face of goal to push away a far-post header from the winger that seemed destined to hit the back of the net.

SAFE HANDS MAN

Bayern Munich's Manuel Neuer is generally considered to be one of the world's best keepers right now, many would say *the* best. In a 2015 Champions League match against Arsenal, the World Cup winner somehow stretched out on the spot to stop a brilliant close-range header from Gunners striker Theo Walcott that was surely going in.

Unfortunately for Neuer, this great save wasn't enough to stop the Gunners winning the match 2-0.

Johnson denied

When the ball arrived at Glen Johnson's feet just six metres from goal in England's EURO 2012 quarter-final against Italy, he was surely going to score. But he hadn't reckoned with Azzurri goalkeeper Gianluigi Buffon. He managed to get an outstretched left hand to Johnson's slightly scooped shot and touched the ball to safety. Johnson couldn't believe it!

Playing in goal can be a thankless task and as every keeper knows, they can pull off a series of sensational saves only to be remembered for just one mistake, misjudgement or mishap.

Costly celebrations

Goalkeepers need to stay calm at all times, as proved by Hans-Jörg Butt during a German league match in 2007. The Bayer Leverkusen star scored from the penalty spot to give his side a 3–1 lead but as he ran back celebrating wildly, Schalke 04 kicked off and Mike Hanke's strike sailed over the distracted goalscoring keeper and into the unguarded net

WORLD CUP CLANGER

There's never a good time to let in a horror goal. England's Robert Green must have wished he hadn't left it until he was at the 2010 World Cup to produce his own moment of madness. With England leading 1–0 against the USA, Green seemed to have Clint Dempsey's hopeful, long-range effort comfortably covered, but rather than bring the weak shot safely into his chest, the keeper let the ball slide off his gloves and roll into the net, gifting the Americans a 1–1 draw.

Robert Green tries to bury his head in the pitch, hoping it will swallow him up.

It's not all bad for the Colombian – Higuita actually scored seven goals for his country during his career!

Maybe Piplica's hairband was tied too tight, making him forget he was a keeper.

HIGUITA'S HORROR

Any goalkeeper who decides to have a dribble outside his area is asking for trouble. That's exactly what Colombia's Rene Higuita, 'El Loco' (the Madman), got at the 1990 World Cup when he attempted an ambitious turn halfway up the pitch, only to be dispossessed by Cameroon's Roger Milla. The African striker strolled gratefully towards the Colombia goal and, despite Higuita's desperate two-footed lunge, slotted home one of the easiest goals of his long and famous career.

On your head

Goalkeepers can be an absent-minded bunch. Bosnian Tomislav Piplica actually forgot goalkeepers are allowed to use their hands in a 2002 Bundesliga clash between Energie Cottbus and Borussia Mönchengladbach. Watching an opponent's volley deflect high into the air, his desperate team-mates screamed "Catch it!" but the hapless goalie bizarrely allowed the ball to bounce off his head and into the goal.

Some footballers love to show off. They can't resist trying a fancy new trick or a cheeky joke to entertain the crowd and the millions of television viewers. Here are a few examples of how some make the most of their moment in the spotlight.

Worse still, this yellow card was one of a number that left Gazza with a two-match ban.

What a cheek!

Players ripping off their shirt after scoring a goal has become a common sight in football, even though they will be shown a yellow card, but Arsenal defender Sammy Nelson chose a cheekier celebration after scoring against Coventry in 1979. He charged towards the Gunners' fans and pulled down his shorts, much to the delight of the Arsenal supporters.

CARD GAMES

After referee Dougie Smith dropped his notebook during a Scottish Premier League clash between Rangers and Hibernian in 1995, Paul Gascoigne noticed the careless official had left his yellow card on the pitch. The midfield prankster promptly showed Smith the card to the amusement of the crowd, but the grumpy ref failed to see the joke, grabbed his card back and immediately booked Gascoigne.

CENSORED!

Sammy Nelson wasn't laughing when Arsenal fined him two weeks' wages.

Seal of disapproval

Showing off can hurt, as Cruzeiro midfielder Kerlon found when he tried out his 'seal dribble' in 2007. He flicked the ball up and repeatedly bounced it on his forehead as he ran past the opposition. Atlético Madrid's Diego Rocha brought his antics to an abrupt end with a hefty forearm smash, receiving a red card and a 120-day ban, while Kerlon got a very sore jaw.

We still don't know who picked up the bill for Šašić's dry cleaning.

SURPRISE SHOWER

It's a brave player that tips a drink over the head of their boss, but that didn't seem to worry an overexcited Olcay Şahan when he began the celebrations after Duisberg's DFB Cup semi-final win over Energie Cottbus in 2011. Judging by the look on Milan Šašić's face, he certainly wasn't expecting to get a shower on the pitch, but at least he was wearing a tracksuit rather than an expensive suit!

Naughty nutmegs and tremendous tricks can light up even the most boring of matches and even though you won't often find them in the coaching books, they are skills which supporters all over the world just can't get enough of.

Mexican magic

Mexican winger Cuauhtémoc Blanco lit up the 1998 World Cup with a sparkling, kangaroo-like move. The cheeky wide man would wedge the ball between his feet, leap between his open-mouthed opponents and then release the ball before hitting the ground and sprinting clear.

THE SCORPION

Rene 'The Madman' Higuita certainly lived up to his billing in 1995 with an unbelievable 'scorpion kick' when Colombia played England at Wembley. England's Jamie Redknapp looped a harmless-looking shot towards the goal, but rather than taking the safe option of just catching the ball, Higuita leapt forwards and cleared the danger in mid-air with the heels of both boots.

Blanco repeated this move several times and it became known as the 'Blanco Bounce'.

Higuita repeated the kick 20 years later, but this time it was into a swimming pool!

ÖZIL'S GUM TRICK

Arsenal's Mesut Özil has wowed his fans with some superb trickery and skill on the pitch. But in a 2013 match against Swansea City, the German World Cup winner showed an unusual skill while warming up on the touchline. He spat out his chewing gum and then, keepie-uppie style, flicked it back up with his boot and into his mouth! Yuck (but cool!).

The ball sticks to Özil's feet like… chewing gum!

Rooney nutmegged

When Nike were filming a TV advert in 2009, the star of the show was meant to be Wayne Rooney but it was actually a 19-year-old by the name of Callam Gardner who grabbed the glory, nutmegging the England star during a five-a-side game and almost ruining the striker's reputation overnight.

Thierry's tricks

Harry Houdini was an escape artist, famous for getting out of seemingly impossible situations. Arsenal's Thierry Henry must have been studying Harry's tricks, judging from a fantastic bit of skill in 2004. He nutmegged Middlesbrough's Danny Mills by the flag and danced past the bemused defender, who thought he had him safely trapped in the corner.

Football is a passionate game, and many people get very hot and bothered about it – players, managers, match officials, supporters – everyone! Here are some examples of moments of madness on the pitch.

MAGPIES MELEE

Newcastle United team-mates Kieron Dyer and Lee Bowyer exchanged punches rather than passes during a defeat to Aston Villa in 2005. Losing 3–0 and already down to ten men, the midfielders suddenly went for each other in front of 50,000 stunned fans at St James' Park, and both collected a red card for their trouble.

Paolo's push

Premier League star Paolo di Canio was as famous for his fiery temper as he was for scoring goals, and his meltdown for Sheffield Wednesday against Arsenal in 1998 is the stuff of legend. After referee Paul Alcock had shown him a red card, the angry Italian shoved him in the chest, causing the most comical stumble and fall in football history. Alcock wobbled, staggered and eventually fell backwards on to the turf while di Canio was handed an 11-match ban for his crime.

Dyer said later that their manager Graeme Souness offered to fight both of them!

South American football is no stranger to mass brawls, but the 2011 Argentinian Fifth Division clash between Claypole and Victoriano broke new ground when referee Damian Rubino sent off a world-record 36 players, substitutes and coaching staff after a huge on-pitch battle broke out in the second half.

Feeble fight

In 2007, Sevilla's Luis Fabiano and Real Zaragoza's Carlos Diogo had the most embarrassing 'punch-up' ever witnessed in La Liga. After going nose-to-nose, the pathetic pair embarked on a hilarious bout of powder-puff punching that saw no one come remotely close to landing a meaningful blow. When he managed to stop laughing, the referee booked the pair of them.

RED MIST OF ZIDANE

Perhaps the most infamous (and stupid) red card in football history came when France's Zinedine Zidane got his marching orders in extra-time of the 2006 World Cup final. With the ball miles away, the fiery playmaker – in his final game before retiring – headbutted the chest of Italy's Marco Materazzi. As he enjoyed his early soak in the bath, France were losing to the Italians in a penalty shoot-out.

Zinedine Zidane looks ready to follow up with his fist!

25

CHAPTER 2
ALL ABOUT THE PLAYERS

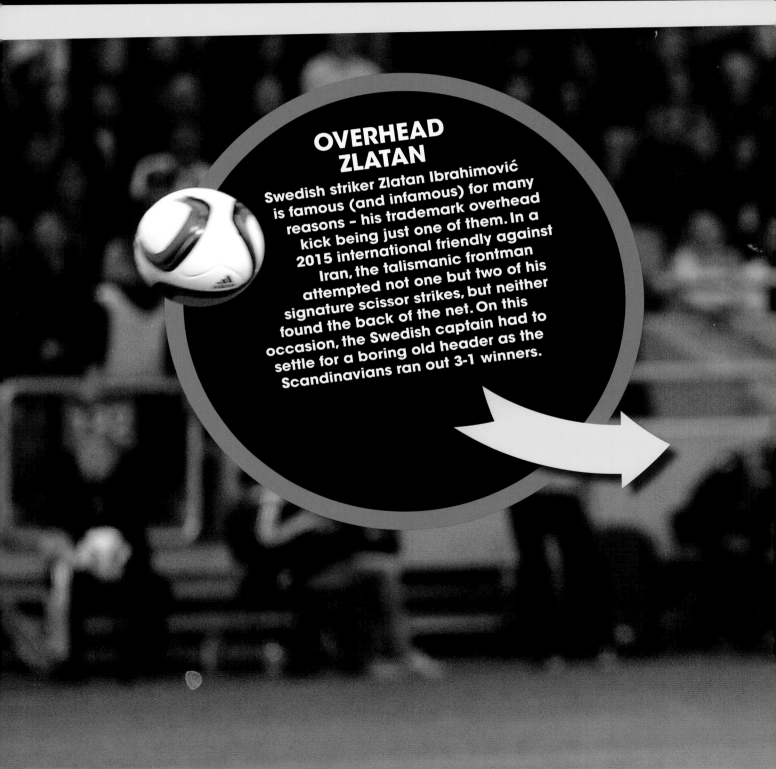

OVERHEAD ZLATAN

Swedish striker Zlatan Ibrahimović is famous (and infamous) for many reasons – his trademark overhead kick being just one of them. In a 2015 international friendly against Iran, the talismanic frontman attempted not one but two of his signature scissor strikes, but neither found the back of the net. On this occasion, the Swedish captain had to settle for a boring old header as the Scandinavians ran out 3-1 winners.

Footballers come in many shapes and sizes. Most are model professionals but a few prefer to stand out from the crowd and act just a little bit different. This chapter pays tribute to the players who don't follow the rules, the wonderful characters who provide almost as much entertainment off the pitch as they do on it.

Preparing themselves for 90 minutes of action can make footballers do the funniest things. Whether it's at home, on the way to the match or inside the stadium itself, it's amazing just what goes on before that first whistle blows.

Petrol Pepe

Most pre-match rituals take place inside the sanctuary of the stadium but Spanish international Pepe Reina used to go to his local petrol station – he would refuse to play for Liverpool unless his petrol tank was full to the brim before kick-off.

Mascorro tries to remember the first-aid training he learned at boy scouts.

MAD MASCORRO

Mexican defender Oscar Mascorro's pre-match is obsessive to say the least. He begins a matchday by getting out of bed on the right-hand side, making sure that his right foot always touches the ground first. He always eats a hamburger, vanilla milkshake and apple juice and then applies bandages to both wrists. On the bandages, he scribbles the letters M & P (the Spanish for mother and father), his own name and his girlfriend's surname. Once finally on the pitch, he digs up a piece of turf and prays for good luck. Phew!

IT STARTED WITH A KISS

During the 1998 World Cup, France skipper Laurent Blanc got into the unusual habit of kissing his goalkeeper's bald head before kick-off. And it wasn't just a quick peck either, with Blanc grabbing his team-mate and giving him a long smooch before every match. Nobody knows why Fabien Barthez allowed it to happen, but it worked wonders as France went on to be crowned world champions.

Blanc thought he was actually kissing the match ball for luck…

Gut feeling

In order to psyche himself up, Dutch legend Johan Cruyff insisted on slapping Ajax keeper Gert Bals as hard as he could across the stomach before each match. Cruyff also spat his chewing gum into the opposition's half seconds before kick-off. The one time he forgot his gum, Ajax lost 4–1 to AC Milan in the final of the 1969 European Cup.

29

Modern footballers are well known for earning a fortune, but before turning professional and picking up their huge pay cheques, plenty of players came from far more modest (and less wealthy) backgrounds.

FISTS OF FURY

Wayne Rooney spent most of his childhood with a football at his feet, but the future England star still found time to pull on a pair of gloves and do boxing training at his local gym. He was a decent fighter, but gave it up at the age of 15 when his first club Everton told him to concentrate on scoring goals rather than walloping people. He has occasionally forgotten that during his subsequent football career...

At the dogs

David Beckham is a multi-millionaire thanks to his wages from football, sponsorship deals and clothing range, but before joining Manchester United as a teenager, the megastar worked at his local greyhound track. "I always remember my time working at Walthamstow dogs," he said. "I picked up glasses at the track. It was my first job and I was so happy to be getting a wage for the first time."

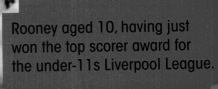

Rooney aged 10, having just won the top scorer award for the under-11s Liverpool League.

Little Lionel

Argentinian superstar Lionel Messi was so tiny as a child that doctors told him he needed treatment if he was going to grow big enough to play professionally. His club River Plate could not afford to pay for the necessary medicine, so Barcelona offered to foot the medical bill. The rest, as they say, is history.

Here's Lionel, looking just like the kid who would get picked last...

Tough life

Maverick goal machine Zlatan Ibrahimović had a tough time growing up in the Swedish city of Malmö. He stole the bike that he used to get to training, and he developed his skills playing street football on a makeshift pitch. Still, it worked out okay for him in the end!

Here's a young, fresh-faced Zlatan while playing for his hometown club, Malmö.

Football fans love to wear their team's replica kit with real pride. But sometimes, the club or country comes up with a design that's so hideous that not even the most loyal fan would be seen dead in it.

COLOUR CLASH

The England goalkeeper's kit from 1995 and 1996 was quite something. Most infamously worn by David Seaman in the semi-final of EURO '96 against Germany, the shirt was a crazy montage of purple, green, yellow and red. Unfortunately for England, it wasn't dazzling enough to make the German players miss in the dramatic penalty shoot-out.

WARNING! Don't look at David for more than 10 seconds as he may give you a headache.

In the pink

Pink is not a colour that is traditionally associated with football. So why Everton decided to wear a bright pink shirt complete with a pair of elephants on the chest for their away games in the 2010–11 Premier League is anyone's guess.

Phil Neville and Leighton Baines congratulate Tim Cahill for scoring despite wearing a hideous pink top.

This strip was probably designed by the guy in the brown suit. That's why he's laughing!

Crazy Campos

Jorge Campos was Mexico's first-choice goalkeeper for much of the 1990s. He bizarrely insisted on designing his own kit for games. The result was a series of horrendous and painfully bright shirts that were guaranteed to induce a blinding headache in any opposition player or fan unwise enough to look in Campos' direction for more than a minute.

COLORADO CALAMITY

An American team called the Colorado Caribous took to the field in 1978 in a weird white, beige and black kit, complete with hilarious leather tassels around the midriff. The cowboy-style football shirt didn't do the Colorado players any favours, as the team slumped to 22 defeats and was disbanded at the end of the season.

Footballers enjoy a lot of free time. Sadly, many of them spend it cultivating some of the most outrageous, gravity-defying and simply ridiculous hairstyles the game has ever seen.

Bleached beard

Portugal's Abel Xavier had nearly as many outlandish haircuts during his career as the games he played. The defender, who had spells at Everton and Liverpool during a four-year stint in the English Premier League, is best known for an eye-catching combo of bleached-blonde flat top and beard!

Valderrama is a hairy hero in Colombia, capped 111 times for the national team.

Abel Xavier's crimes against bleach didn't stop Portugal reaching the semi-finals of EURO 2000.

Carlos' crazy curls

Colombian midfielder Carlos Valderrama sported one of the biggest hairdos in football history. His tight corkscrew perm was dyed blonde and so huge he could have stashed the World Cup in there and no one would have been any the wiser.

A team to dye for

At the 1998 World Cup, Romania astonished the crowd at their group game against Tunisia when the entire team emerged from the tunnel with bleached-blonde hair. The stunt was to celebrate qualifying for the knockout stages with a win over England in the previous game. All that dye must have gone to their heads – they were dumped out in the next round by Croatia.

Green and mean

Standing over six feet tall, it was difficult to miss Nigeria's Taribo West. But the big defender made sure he wasn't overlooked by sporting one of football's most unusual hairstyles. For almost his entire 15-year career, he kept most of his head shaved bald, dying the remaining locks green and plaiting them together into antenna-like bunches!

DOUBLE BUBBLES

Belgium hit the hairdressing headlines at the 2014 World Cup thanks to the matching bubble perms of hotshot midfielders Marouane Fellaini and Axel Witsel. "If we win the World Cup, I'll shave my head," claimed Fellaini. The team fell short, knocked out by Argentina in the quarter-finals, but Fellaini went ahead anyway, and the most famous hairdo in world football was – briefly – no more.

Fellaini's gravity-defying curls were soon back with full force. Axel Witsel (right) looks impressed.

TALL AND SHORT

In the beautiful game, size is no obstacle to participation and whether you're ridiculously big or surprisingly small, anyone can pull on their pair of boots, emerge from the dressing room and play a match.

When Aarøy couldn't get the ball, he just reached down and lifted players out of the way!

GIANTS OF BRAZIL

Brazilians have always been big in the football world but the country also boasts the planet's smallest team. With an average height of just 1.2m, the side is made up of dwarves from northeast Brazil. Refusing to take themselves too seriously, they're called 'Gigantes do Norte' (Giants of the North) and they take on local Under-13 teams in regular friendly matches.

Gigantes play on regular pitches but are allowed to double up on each other's shoulders to defend free kicks.

SKYSCRAPER STRIKER

Goalkeeper Kristof van Hout might be the tallest footballer around at 2.08m, but Norwegian striker Tor Hogne Aarøy was Europe's tallest outfield player until his recent retirement, standing at 2.04m. He was a complete menace at corners and dead-ball situations.

BELGIAN BIG GUY

It's no great surprise that the world's tallest professional footballer – Kristof van Hout – is a goalkeeper. Taking up most of the goal, the 2.08m Belgian beanpole has earned a reputation as a brilliant penalty saver for Willem II, Standard Liège, Genk and Westerlo. He just needs to be careful not to bang his head on the crossbar.

Van Hout is literally head and shoulders above the competition!

Chinese colossus

It doesn't look pretty, but hoofing the ball high and long onto the head of a massive centre-forward can be very effective. This makes giant strikers a good addition to any side and they don't come any bigger than 2.06m forward Yang Changpeng. Yang made quite an impression while on trial with Bolton Wanderers in 2006, and now looms large over defenders for China League Two team Yinchuan Helanshan.

YOUNG AND OLD

There's a saying in football that if you're good enough, you're old enough. There have been plenty of young footballers past and present who have proved that point, but that doesn't mean the old-timers can't make a difference too...

YOUNG GALACTICO

Norwegian wonder kid Martin Ødegaard became Real Madrid's youngest ever player after making his debut during their final-day clash with Getafe in May 2015. Aged just 16 years and 157 days, he replaced Cristiano Ronaldo in the 58th minute of Madrid's dramatic 7-3 win at the Bernabeu.

Leading from the front

Captains are usually one of the more experienced players in a team, but keeper Tony Meola took the armband for the USA at the 1990 World Cup at the tender age of 21 years, 316 days. He still holds the record for the youngest ever skipper in World Cup history. Peter Shilton became the oldest captain in the finals when he led out England at the same tournament in the third-place play-off against Italy. He was 40 years and 292 days old.

Ødegaard spent most of his first season at Real on the bench, but he still has many years ahead of him!

Staying power

Most professional footballers hang up their boots long before their 40th birthday, but Sir Stanley Matthews was made of strong stuff. He was still playing for Stoke City in the top flight after passing 50. His England career spanned an incredible 23 years and he made nearly 700 Football League appearances between 1932 and 1965.

BOY WONDER

A Bolivian league clash between Aurora and La Paz in 2009 saw history made when 12-year-old Mauricio Baldivieso came on for the final nine minutes of the match, becoming the world's youngest ever professional footballer in the process. Which of course had absolutely nothing whatsoever to do with the fact that the Aurora manager was Baldivieso's dad, Julio.

Young Mauricio waves to the crowd. Probably looking for his mum…

LIONEL'S RECORDS

Midfield maestro Lionel Messi has been rewriting history ever since he broke into the Barcelona first team during the 2004–05 season. One of the first Nou Camp records to fall to the amazing Argentinian was becoming the club's youngest player to score a league goal when he netted in a La Liga clash with Albacete Balompié aged just 17 years, ten months and seven days.

FOOTBALL HEAVYWEIGHTS

Today's professional footballers are meant to be models of athleticism and fitness, but sometimes even the game's greatest players are tempted by the lure of burger and chips, stuffed-crust pizza and double choc-chip ice cream.

Portly Puskás

The late, great Ferenc Puskás loved life and his lifestyle meant the Hungarian legend wasn't exactly as fit as he could have been. When he signed for Real Madrid in 1958, he was 18kg overweight but that didn't stop Puskás scoring an incredible 157 league goals in just 182 games for the club.

Tomas breaks into a trot, having sniffed out a hotdog in the crowd.

TUBBY TOMAS

Tomas Brolin was a lean, mean scoring machine in his younger days in his native Sweden and then in Italy, but he'd transformed into a bit of a lump by the time he signed for Leeds United in 1995. Carrying far too much extra weight, he spectacularly failed to make the grade in the Premier League.

Ronaldo gets rounder

To be fair to Brazilian star Ronaldo, knee injuries blighted the final years of his playing days but the former Barcelona, Inter Milan and Real Madrid striker piled on the pounds and, as a result, quickly if unimaginatively became known as 'Fat Ronaldo' to football fans across the world.

Big Nev

Coaches are always telling their keepers to 'fill the goal' and Everton and Wales legend Neville Southall did exactly what he was told, getting bigger and bigger as each of his 17 seasons passed at Goodison Park. It didn't stop him being one of the finest stoppers of the 1980s and '90s though.

Big Nev holds out his hand to a catch a bar of chocolate thrown from the stands.

GREAT DANE

Jan Mølby was capped 33 times for Denmark and was the creative mastermind of Liverpool's midfield in the 1980s and early 1990s. His bulky figure, together with his silky on-field skills, made him a cult hero, but Molby's career nosedived after he was injured in a match against Manchester United in October 1992. He routinely gained weight when injured and was unable to train, but is still idolized by Anfield fans of a certain age.

Liverpool's sponsor at the time was – appropriately enough – Candy.

CHAPTER 3
BENDING THE RULES

CROSSBAR KARMA

Germany may have been on the wrong end of a goal-line ruling in the 1966 World Cup final, but luck was most definitely on their side in the 2010 World Cup quarter-final against England. Leading 2–1, the Germans thought they'd conceded an equaliser when Frank Lampard's shot hit the crossbar and landed over the line (the TV pictures clearly showed that it did). This time the referee said no and Germany went on to win 4–1.

In the heat of battle, football officials and players can make mistakes. Many games are remembered for controversial decisions, acts of skulduggery or moments of hilarious confusion. Rules, it's said, are made to be broken and in football, players will often take any opportunity to push the laws to their limit.

GOAL OR NO GOAL?

Goal-line technology that proves when the ball crosses the line is now in use in some leagues and competitions, but whenever the game is played without it, there will always be questions about goals that should or should not be allowed.

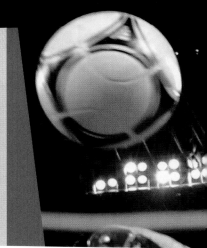

1966 and all that

There will perhaps never be a more controversial goal than the one scored by Geoff Hurst for England against West Germany in extra-time of the 1966 World Cup final. Proud Englishmen will never tire of insisting that Geoff's shot off the crossbar definitely did cross the line, while disgruntled Germans are still cursing linesman Tofiq Bahramov and his terrible eyesight.

Hurst scores the controversial third goal. England eventually won 4-2 after extra-time.

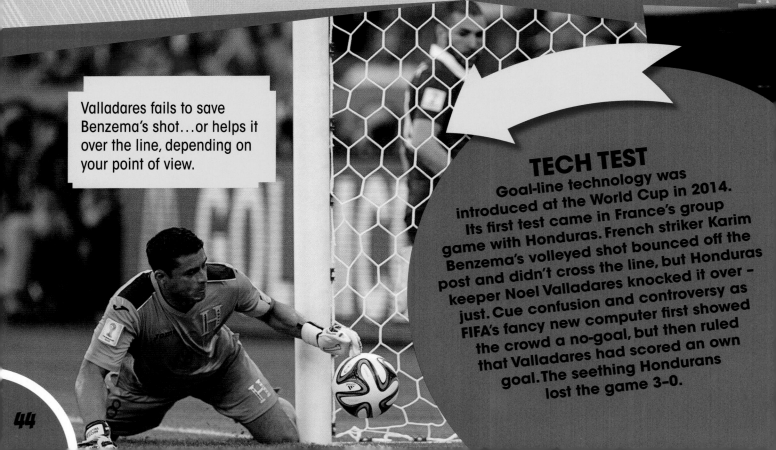

Valladares fails to save Benzema's shot…or helps it over the line, depending on your point of view.

TECH TEST

Goal-line technology was introduced at the World Cup in 2014. Its first test came in France's group game with Honduras. French striker Karim Benzema's volleyed shot bounced off the post and didn't cross the line, but Honduras keeper Noel Valladares knocked it over – just. Cue confusion and controversy as FIFA's fancy new computer first showed the crowd a no-goal, but then ruled that Valladares had scored an own goal. The seething Hondurans lost the game 3–0.

Lucky Liverpool

Former Chelsea manager José Mourinho dubbed himself 'The Special One' but he certainly wasn't The Lucky One when his side faced Liverpool in the semis of the 2005 Champions League. The result was decided by what became known as the 'ghost goal'. TV replays couldn't prove whether or not Luis García's tap-in from close range had crossed the line, but referee Lubos Michel gave the goal, sending Liverpool into the final and Mourinho into meltdown.

DRAWING THE LINE

No major tournament would be complete without a mistake from the match officials, and EURO 2012 was no different. England were again involved when John Terry cleared a shot from Ukraine's Marko Devic in the final group game. Replays proved the ball was over the line but with no video technology, the 'goal' was not given and the Three Lions won 1–0. England's good fortune didn't last long, however, as they followed up their controversial win by losing to Italy on penalties in the quarter-finals.

Terry clears off the line, but the ball was actually over it. Not that the referee saw...

HANDBALL!

Football is – you guessed it – played with the feet. But there are always some players who cannot resist handling the ball. Many do it by accident, while others know exactly what they are doing…

Diego's deception

The most famous handball of all time was in the 1986 World Cup quarter-final. England keeper Peter Shilton jumped to punch away a clearance, but was beaten by the outstretched hand of Argentina's Diego Maradona, who redirected the ball into the net to take a 1-0 lead. But there was no argument over Maradona's second goal, an incredible dribble from the halfway line past four bewildered England players that was voted the Goal of the Century by FIFA.

It's catching!

When Australia hit the post at the 2011 Women's World Cup, no one expected Equatorial Guinea defender Bruna to catch the ball. As the Australians screamed for a penalty, the confused referee simply stood and watched as Bruna finally realized her mistake, dropped the ball and played on as if nothing had happened. Despite not being awarded a penalty, justice was done as the Aussies ran out 3-2 winners.

GHEZZAL'S GOTTA GO

Tunisia's Abdelkader Ghezzal came off the bench for Tunisia against Slovenia at the 2010 World Cup and got booked for shirt-pulling 48 seconds later. It was the quickest yellow card for a sub in World Cup history, but worse was to come. Fifteen minutes later, Ghezzal dived to intercept a pass… with his right arm! A red card followed, and six minutes later Slovenia scored the winner against the understrength Tunisians.

STRIKER TURNS KEEPER

At the 2010 World Cup, Uruguay and Ghana were locked together at 1-1 in the last few seconds of extra-time. When Ghana's Dominic Adiyiah headed towards goal, it looked like a dramatic last-gasp winner... until Uruguay's Luis Suárez punched the ball away. Suárez was sent off, but Ghana missed the penalty and the South Americans went on to win in a penalty shootout.

Luis Suárez takes over goalkeeping duties against Ghana at the World Cup.

Ghezzal's graceful save meant he missed Algeria's 0-0 draw against England.

Two-hands Thierry

France won a 2009 World Cup qualifying play-off against the Republic of Ireland in controversial fashion. With the second leg deadlocked at 1-1 in extra-time, striker Thierry Henry used his hand – twice! – to keep the ball in play before setting up William Gallas for the winner. Henry owned up to the crime, but Irish pleas for a replay fell on deaf ears, and the French headed sheepishly to the finals.

SHOOTOUT SHAME

The dreaded penalty shootout creates instant heroes and villains in equal measure and while it's a favourite with the fans, most players would rather do almost anything else than step up to the spot and try their luck.

BALL INTO SPACE – PART 1

Most professionals agree that the perfect penalty is hit low and hard. Sadly for England, Chris Waddle's sky-high effort from the spot against West Germany in the 1990 World Cup semi-final was anything but. It was this miss which sent the Germans through to the final and so began the Three Lions' infamous run of misery in major shootouts.

BALL INTO SPACE – PART 2

Roberto Baggio was in sensational form for Italy en route to the final of the 1994 World Cup but his luck well and truly ran out in the final shootout, blasting his penalty high and wide to spark wild celebrations on the victorious Brazil bench and much crying among his dejected Italian team-mates.

Waddle can only watch in horror as the ball heads off into orbit.

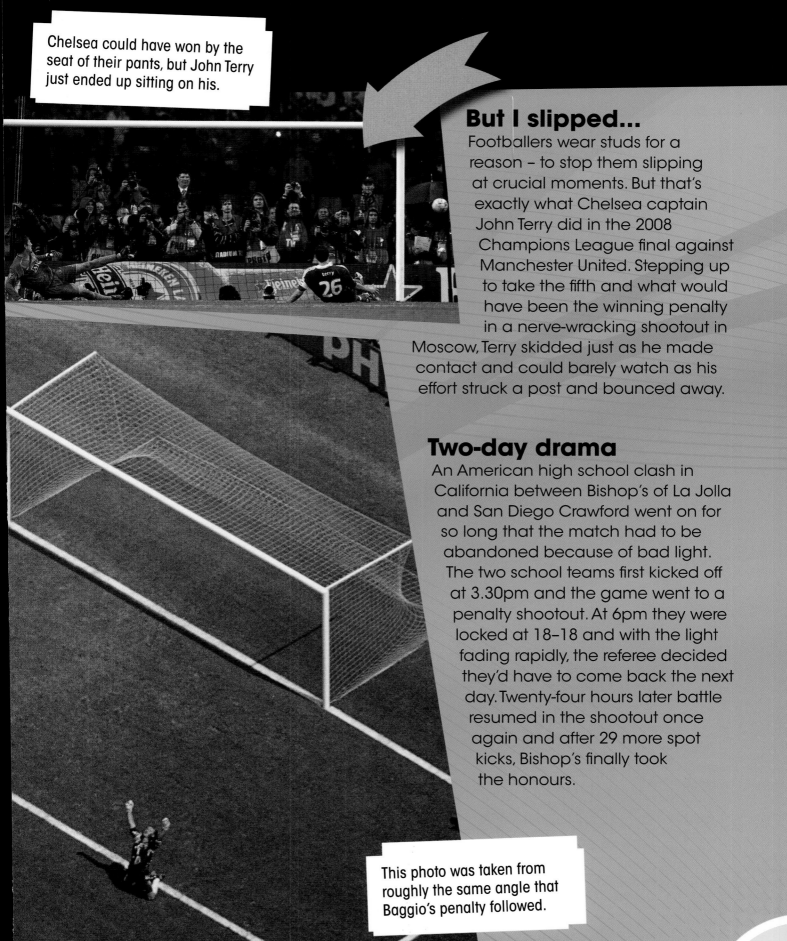

Chelsea could have won by the seat of their pants, but John Terry just ended up sitting on his.

But I slipped...

Footballers wear studs for a reason – to stop them slipping at crucial moments. But that's exactly what Chelsea captain John Terry did in the 2008 Champions League final against Manchester United. Stepping up to take the fifth and what would have been the winning penalty in a nerve-wracking shootout in Moscow, Terry skidded just as he made contact and could barely watch as his effort struck a post and bounced away.

Two-day drama

An American high school clash in California between Bishop's of La Jolla and San Diego Crawford went on for so long that the match had to be abandoned because of bad light. The two school teams first kicked off at 3.30pm and the game went to a penalty shootout. At 6pm they were locked at 18–18 and with the light fading rapidly, the referee decided they'd have to come back the next day. Twenty-four hours later battle resumed in the shootout once again and after 29 more spot kicks, Bishop's finally took the honours.

This photo was taken from roughly the same angle that Baggio's penalty followed.

We all know that the offside law can be hard to understand, but you'd think that the officials would get it right at least. Sadly, faced with having to keep their eyes on the ball and keeping the players under control, even the pros can make mistakes.

FOUR OFFSIDE

Schalke 04's Joël Matip could barely believe his luck when he scored his team's second goal in a 2013 Champions League win over Basel. Not only was Matip blatantly offside, but at least THREE of his team-mates were, too. The linesman who gave the goal was clearly asleep or had his eyes closed. Or maybe he wasn't even at the game!

HANDS UP

If you're going to appeal for offside, it can be a good idea for the whole team to do it at the same time. That's exactly what Newcastle United did in a Premier League clash with Manchester United in November 2011. Their synchronised show of hands worked a treat and persuaded the linesman to rule out Javier Hernández's goal.

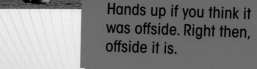

Hands up if you think it was offside. Right then, offside it is.

Matip's team-mates look on as he scores a goal that should never have been.

Brolly bust-up

Standing alone on the edge of the pitch isn't always a pleasant experience for linesmen, especially when the crowd doesn't agree with their decisions. Unfortunately, assistant referee Javier Aguilar Rodriguez found this out when he was hit by a flying umbrella thrown from the terraces during a 2011 Spanish Primera Liga clash between Granada and Majorca. His face was cut and referee Carlos Clos Gómez took pity, ordering everyone off the pitch and abandoning the game.

Whistle woe

'Playing to the whistle' is one of football's most famous clichés but Kuwait took the saying a little too literally in their 1982 World Cup clash with France. The entire team heard a shrill blast and stopped playing, assuming the referee had blown for offside. The problem was the referee hadn't actually made a sound, but France took full advantage and promptly scored. Chaos ensued as the Kuwaiti officials stormed the pitch in protest. The intervention of Prince Fahid of Kuwait finally persuaded the ref to disallow the goal.

STRICTLY COME DIVING

Considering football is played almost exclusively with your feet, it's remarkable how hard some players find it to stay on them. Sometimes it seems that the slightest touch can send them crashing to the ground and they want us to believe they're hurt when it's far from the truth.

Meier's madness

Managers are meant to set a good example to their players but Duisburg boss Norbert Meier did the opposite in 2005 when he stopped Cologne midfielder Albert Streit from taking a quick throw-in. The pair squared up to each other, and after the faintest of touches of the forehead, both men flung themselves backwards as if they'd been kicked by a black-belt karate fighter.

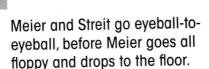

Meier and Streit go eyeball-to-eyeball, before Meier goes all floppy and drops to the floor.

DROPPIN' ROBBEN

Dutch master wingman Arjen Robben has loads of pace, sublime dribbling skills and can cross the ball with amazing accuracy. He can also fall to the ground at the drop of a hat – and beat the hat on the way. In the Netherlands' Round of 16 match against Mexico in the 2014 World Cup, Robben spectacularly fell to the ground in a sort of 'double-flop' after being challenged by Rafael Marquez. The resulting penalty was scored, and to make matters worse, Robben even admitted afterwards that he dived.

Drogba goes down in typical style in the 2005 FA Community Shield against Arsenal.

Blow me down

Despite being a big, strong lad, Didier Drogba has a reputation as being, let's say, a little unstable on his feet. For every goal the Ivory Coast striker has scored in his career, there has been an incident when he's suddenly hit the turf and fallen over like a very large sack of potatoes.

THE ANTI-DIVE

Footballers aren't always all bad. In 1997, Liverpool striker Robbie Fowler showed his honesty after he stumbled over Arsenal goalie David Seaman and was awarded a penalty. Fowler signalled to ref Gerald Ashby that he should not award a spot kick. Despite this, the official forced Liverpool to take the penalty and although Fowler's kick was saved, Jason McAteer banged in the rebound. Fowler was rewarded later though when he was handed a Fair Play Award by UEFA.

Marquez is saying, "Sorry about that Arjen, let me help you up." Or not.

Life as a football referee is rarely easy, and sooner or later they will make a mistake. Unfortunately for the game's officials, as they're outnumbered in a stadium by players and the crowd, what happens next is totally out of their control.

Dangerous Dane

Awarding a penalty is often controversial, but as German ref Herbert Fandel learned in 2007, it can be dangerous too. In charge of a Denmark v Sweden EURO 2008 qualifier in Copenhagen, Fandel sent off a Danish defender and gave the visitors a late spot kick, prompting Danish fan Ronni Norvig to invade the pitch and try to punch him. Luckily for the referee, a Danish player stepped in to save him. The game was abandoned, Sweden were awarded a 3–0 win and Norvig fined a hefty £210,000.

Yellow peril

Everyone knows that two yellow cards equal a sending-off. Everyone that is except English referee Graham Poll, who disastrously decided to rip up the rulebook at the 2006 World Cup in Germany. He showed Croatia's Josip Šimunić three yellows before finally giving him marching orders against Australia. Only Poll knows why he didn't send Šimunić off after his second yellow.

Norvig ended up paying only £30,000 and has since "fallen out of love with football".

PERFECT PIERLUIGI

The most famous referee of his generation, Pierluigi Collina was as distinctive looking as he was strict. The Italian reached the peak of his profession when he took charge of the 2002 World Cup final between Brazil and Germany. Collina now trains the next generation of Italian whistlers, as well as appearing in TV adverts but not, we assume, for hair products.

Collina breaks out his trademark stare during a match between Greece and the Czech Republic at EURO 2004.

Play-offs are always tense, and so it was when France took on the Republic of Ireland in the second-leg of a play-off where the prize was a spot at the 2010 World Cup. Irish fans will never forgive or forget Swedish referee Martin Hansson, who failed to spot Thierry Henry handling the ball twice in the build-up to the goal that sent France through 2-1. Henry even admitted handling it afterwards and said, "I am not the ref..."

The Irish players are most definitely not about to give the referee a hug.

Card crazy

The Portugal v Netherlands 2006 World Cup tie was always going to be interesting, but Russian ref Valentin Ivanov made it crazy! In a game of only 25 fouls, he showed Mark van Bommel a yellow card after two minutes and Khalid Boulahrouz one five minutes later. By the final whistle, the yellow-card count was at 16, with two players from each side sent off after receiving two cautions. Portugal's Maniche was careful to keep his shirt on after scoring the only goal – just as well, seeing as he'd already been booked once.

Liverpool boss Jürgen Klopp has always been a favourite with fans. Here, he even gets a hug from his opponents' mascot – Aston Villa's Hercules the Lion.

The action out on the pitch is only part of the big-match experience for supporters. So the next time you're bored at a game, keep your eyes peeled and whether it's a sudden bolt of lightning, an over-enthusiastic police dog or a furry animal punch-up, you never know what might happen next.

MASCOT MAD

Club mascots are an essential part of the match-day experience. What game wouldn't be complete without a brightly coloured, oversized furry creature running up and down the touchline to delight (or terrify) the younger fans? Arsenal's Gunnersaurus and Bayern Munich's Berni the Bear are near-megastars in their own right. The north London dino has over 15,000 Twitter followers, while Berni accompanies Bayern everywhere they go, often making the news as much as the team.

WEATHER WARNING

Football is traditionally an outdoor sport, which means players and supporters often find themselves at the mercy of Mother Nature and her array of extreme climatic conditions. It's little wonder then that so many matches over the years have had to bow down to the power of the natural world.

WIND OF CHANGE

Footballers occasionally have to duck and dive to avoid objects thrown at them by idiots in the crowd, but the officials and players of the Black Leopards and Orlando Pirates in South Africa were faced by a far greater threat in 2007 when strong winds starting blowing the hoardings at Ellis Park, Johannesburg, onto the pitch.

Storm stops play

They say a little rain never hurt anyone but when it's accompanied by terrifying bolts of lightning and enormous claps of thunder, it's wise not to take any chances. That's what UEFA decided when an apocalyptic storm engulfed Donetsk moments after the start of Ukraine's match with France at EURO 2012. The players took refuge in the dressing rooms while the fans huddled at the back of the stands for shelter. The game resumed after a 55-minute delay.

Some players are accused of dropping to the floor for no reason, but they had a good excuse here!

SWIMMING LESSONS

In Brazil in 2011, Sao Paulo's match with Palmeiras witnessed such a torrential downpour that the fans were literally swimming in the water-filled stands of the Morumbi Stadium before kick-off. Rivers of water flowing down through the terraces quickly filled the bottom rows of seats, but amazingly the match still went ahead after a 70-minute delay – only for another interruption in the second half when the water got into the electrics and caused a floodlight failure.

The only match in which rain stopped play but allowed for a swimming competition in its place.

SHAKE, RATTLE & ROLL

Manchester United's pre-season tour of the Far East in 2005 took a frightening turn in Japan when they played the Kashima Antlers in Tokyo – an earthquake rocked the National Stadium! The surprise tremor came midway through the second half and once the United players worked out it wasn't Sir Alex Ferguson shouting at them from the touchline, they realised it had to be an earthquake. The Antlers won the game 2–1.

AMAZING STADIUMS

Whether a club is big or small, there really is no place like its home stadium. But not all grounds are the same and as the following examples prove, even football stadiums can have unusual and sometimes unbelievable claims to fame…

On the water

Some would argue that today's football superstars think they can walk on water and if they played a game at The Float at Marina Bay in Singapore, they literally could. A floating platform measuring 118m by 82m, The Float can hold up to 30,000 spectators and staged its first match in 2009 when Tuan Gemuk Athletic and VNNTU FC donned their armbands for a Sunday League ESPZEN amateur match.

GREEN AGENDA

The grass is usually the greenest thing inside a football ground but the Estádio Janguito Malucelli in Brazil is the exception. Not a drop of concrete or an ounce of metal was used to build it. Nicknamed the 'Brazil Eco-Stadium', its main stand was built on a hill, with the seating cut out of the earth and only recycled wood was used for the changing rooms and other buildings.

It must be fun for the ground staff when they have to mow the stand.

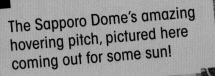

The Sapporo Dome's amazing hovering pitch, pictured here coming out for some sun!

COLOUR CO-ORDINATED

The Allianz Arena in Bavaria hosts games for both Bayern Munich and TSV 1860 München, and the ground's designers came up with a clever plan to make both teams feel at home. An innovative lighting system on the outside of the stadium makes it red when Bayern play and blue when TSV 1860 have a game. It even glows white when the German national team are in town.

Sliding sensation

A good sliding tackle can be a beautiful sight, but at the super high-tech Sapporo Dome in Japan, it's the entire pitch that does the sliding. Built for the 2002 World Cup, the stadium boasts a retractable, 8,300-tonne pitch which can slide in and out of the Dome to expose the turf to sunlight when the weather is good. It can also be turned 90 degrees to improve the view for spectators, depending on whether it's staging football or baseball.

Allianz Arena

The Allianz Arena glows red for Bayern before a Champions League match against Olympiacos.

MORE AMAZING STADIUMS

Slide and rise

The Stade Pierre Mauroy in the French city of Lille is home to the city's Ligue 1 club. It has a sliding roof like many high-tech modern stadiums, but its pitch is unique. Half of it can lift up and slide across the other half, revealing a secret smaller venue used to host events such as basketball, tennis and music concerts.

Let's hope the pitch stays put when the games are being played!

Monaco maths

Getting tickets to the big match can sometimes be a problem for fans, but supporters who want to watch Monaco play in the French league rarely have to worry about getting into the game. The team plays at the Stade Louis II, which has a capacity of 18,500, while the Principality of Monaco is home to 36,000 people – meaning more than half of the country's entire population can cram into the ground at the same time for hotdogs, swearing at the referee and some football.

SHAKING STADIUM

The metal poles of the Nouveau Stade de Bordeaux in France are designed to resemble pine trees in the nearby forests. A host venue for EURO 2016, this stunning new stadium seats 42,000 fans, with some of the upper seating at a dizzying 35-degree angle. What's more, this near all-metal structure tends to vibrate a bit when the fans get excited and jump about. Woah!

Rumour has it, if the fans all jump at the right time, the stadium plays the French national anthem.

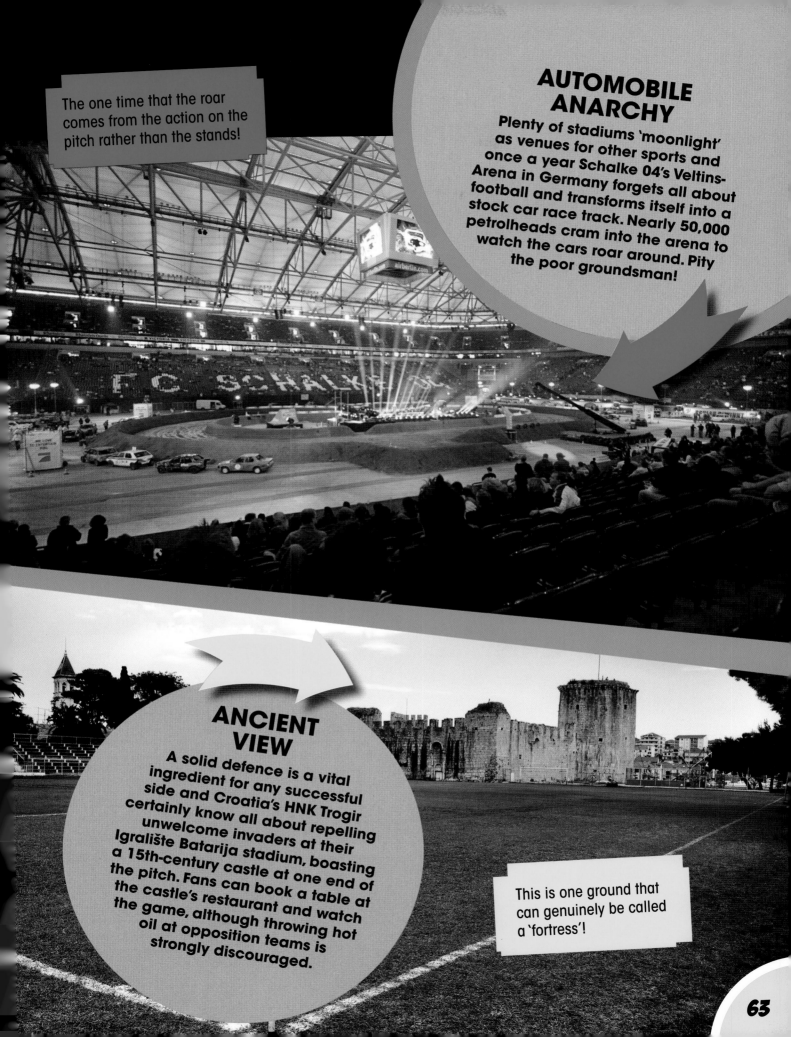

The one time that the roar comes from the action on the pitch rather than the stands!

AUTOMOBILE ANARCHY

Plenty of stadiums 'moonlight' as venues for other sports and once a year Schalke 04's Veltins-Arena in Germany forgets all about football and transforms itself into a stock car race track. Nearly 50,000 petrolheads cram into the arena to watch the cars roar around. Pity the poor groundsman!

ANCIENT VIEW

A solid defence is a vital ingredient for any successful side and Croatia's HNK Trogir certainly know all about repelling unwelcome invaders at their Igralište Batarija stadium, boasting a 15th-century castle at one end of the pitch. Fans can book a table at the castle's restaurant and watch the game, although throwing hot oil at opposition teams is strongly discouraged.

This is one ground that can genuinely be called a 'fortress'!

ANIMAL ANTICS

Football and the animal world do not usually mix and judging by these bizarre, often painful and frequently funny incidents, it's something that both football and our furry and feathered friends should try and keep that way.

Run, rabbit! Run!

The Spanish word for rabbit is 'conejo' and that's what the players of Real Madrid and Real Betis all shouted in 1997 when one of the big-eared fellas was thrown from the stands at the Bernabeu. The players gave chase and it was Madrid's Carlos Secretario who caught the roaming rabbit. "Secretario may or may be not a good player," joked the match commentator, "but he is indeed a great hunter."

Benito is seen here making a grab for the little critter, just before it bites him!

SWISS PINE

It's rare to see a pine marten, even in the woods and forests where they live. So it was even more of a surprise to see one on the pitch during a 2013 Swiss Super League game between FC Thun and Zurich. Play was suspended as the nippy critter ran around the ground, into the stands and back on to the turf. Eventually, Zurich defender Loris Benito grabbed it, only for the furry intruder to bite him on the finger. Ouch!

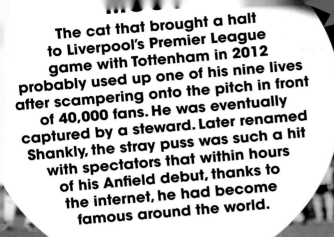

The cat that brought a halt to Liverpool's Premier League game with Tottenham in 2012 probably used up one of his nine lives after scampering onto the pitch in front of 40,000 fans. He was eventually captured by a steward. Later renamed Shankly, the stray puss was such a hit with spectators that within hours of his Anfield debut, thanks to the internet, he had become famous around the world.

Not to be outdone by their local rivals, Everton acquired a feline friend of their own when this moggy ran onto the pitch during an FA Cup tie in 2016.

Bovine bother

Most animals that invade the pitch get there by accident, but the two cows who grazed the grass at the Amsterdam Arena in the Netherlands in 2001 were put there on purpose – by the club's own fans. After the Arena turf was replaced 24 times in just five years, the supporters were so fed up with the playing surface that they sent out the cows in protest.

It took a lot to beat the legendary Kahn, but this wasp managed it!

Stung into action

Bored goalkeepers are usually grateful for any distraction to liven a dull 90 minutes, but Bayern Munich stopper Oliver Kahn could have done without the wasp sting that had him writhing in agony in a cup clash with Werder Bremen in 2007. Officials thought Kahn had been hit by a missile thrown from the stands, but the penny dropped when the angry Bayern star asked for a can of insecticide and a rolled-up newspaper.

65

CHAPTER 5
MEET THE BOSS

PEP'S THE BEST

Managers are some of football's great characters, larger-than-life figures who take the flak when things go wrong and who are often only a defeat away from losing their jobs. Spanish coach Josep 'Pep' Guardiola is one of the most sought-after managers in the modern game. At Barcelona, he won an incredible 14 trophies in four seasons, including a Champions League win in 2009 that made him the youngest manager ever to win the competition. After a successful spell at Bayern Munich, Guardiola secured a move to the Premier League in 2016, where he succeeded Manuel Pellegrini at Manchester City.

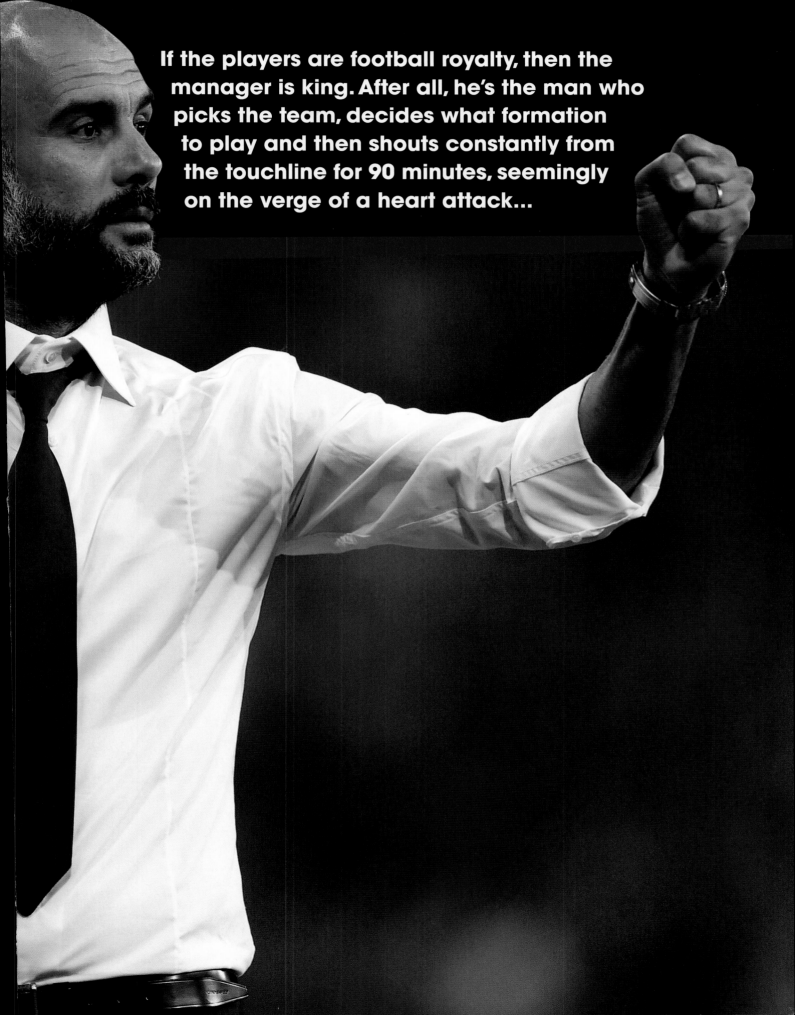

If the players are football royalty, then the manager is king. After all, he's the man who picks the team, decides what formation to play and then shouts constantly from the touchline for 90 minutes, seemingly on the verge of a heart attack...

Some people say you have to be mad to be a goalie, but it's possibly football's managers who need their heads examining! Under constant pressure and often facing the sack, it should come as no surprise that they occasionally go a little bit crazy...

Air play

First impressions always count and Swedish legend Pia Sundhage created quite a stir when she took over as manager of the USA Women's team in 2007. Speaking to her squad for the first time, Sundhage played air guitar and began singing. The ever-smiling Swede even played her imaginary guitar on the touchline during the 2011 World Cup in Germany.

Mourinho is seen here laughing at the beginning of the 2015-16 season, but the smiles didn't last long...

THE SPECIAL ONE

José Mourinho is one of the most successful coaches in the modern game – and he knows it. He shot to fame after winning the Champions League with FC Porto in 2004 before joining Chelsea and delivering their first league title for 50 years. When he first joined Chelsea, he famously said: "Please don't call me arrogant but I'm European champion and I think I'm a special one." Mourinho refuses to change his style, but his second spell at Chelsea wasn't quite so special, and after a string of defeats he left under a cloud in December 2015.

Brian Clough was one of the best English managers but he was also slightly bonkers. Known as 'Old Big 'Ead' because of he was always talking himself up, Clough would say things like, "I wouldn't say I was the best manager in the business but I was in the top one" and "Rome wasn't built in a day but I wasn't on that particular job." He tortured his players with constant wisecracks but got the very best out of them, especially at Nottingham Forest, winning back-to-back European Cups in 1979 and 1980.

Clough is shown here playing cricket in his underpants. As you do…

KOP'S KLOPP

Jürgen Klopp arrived at Liverpool in 2015 as something of a fan favourite. Known for his sense of humour, floppy hair and designer glasses, he can always be relied on for a great quote. Comparing himself to José Mourinho, he said he was 'the normal one', and of his rival at Arsenal: "Wenger likes having the ball, playing football, passes… like an orchestra… I like heavy metal."

Jürgen treats the Liverpool fans to a typical goofy smile!

Old-fashioned wooden benches may now have been replaced by luxury leather armchairs and plastic roofs, but the dugout is still the manager's domain and it remains a hotbed of raw emotion, comic capers and furious fights!

Sausage subs

Football clubs are always looking at new ways to make money but few have been as forward thinking as Spanish club Sevilla, who accepted loads of Euros from a local meat company in 2012 in return for remodelling their dugout as a giant hot dog. The roof became the sausage, complete with twirls of ketchup and mustard, while the back of the bench was transformed into the bun. It looked bizarre and probably made the crowd more hungry than usual.

Sleepy head

It's understandable when substitutes lose interest in a game, especially when they've got no chance of actually kicking a ball in anger – but falling asleep is just asking for trouble. Just ask Real Madrid's Julien Faubert, who was so bored by his side's 3–2 victory over Villarreal in 2009 that he decided to grab 40 winks during the game. Perhaps he was dreaming of making a rare appearance for the team?

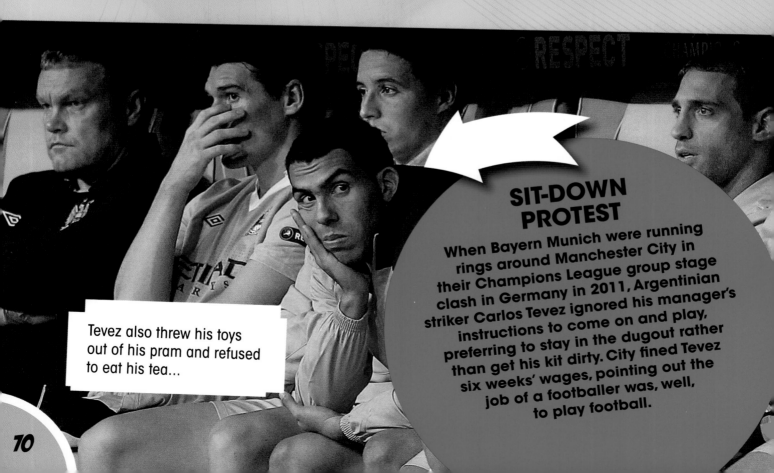

Tevez also threw his toys out of his pram and refused to eat his tea...

SIT-DOWN PROTEST

When Bayern Munich were running rings around Manchester City in their Champions League group stage clash in Germany in 2011, Argentinian striker Carlos Tevez ignored his manager's instructions to come on and play, preferring to stay in the dugout rather than get his kit dirty. City fined Tevez six weeks' wages, pointing out the job of a footballer was, well, to play football.

"Both of you can go and sit on the naughty step!"

IT'S MY BALL!

Roberto Mancini is usually very calm but the supercool Italian totally lost the plot when manager of Manchester City during a 2010 Premier League clash with Everton. After his opposite number David Moyes refused to give the ball back, Mancini began tussling with Moyes on the touchline! Their little game was brought to an abrupt end when referee Peter Walton told them both to grow up and sent them to the stands.

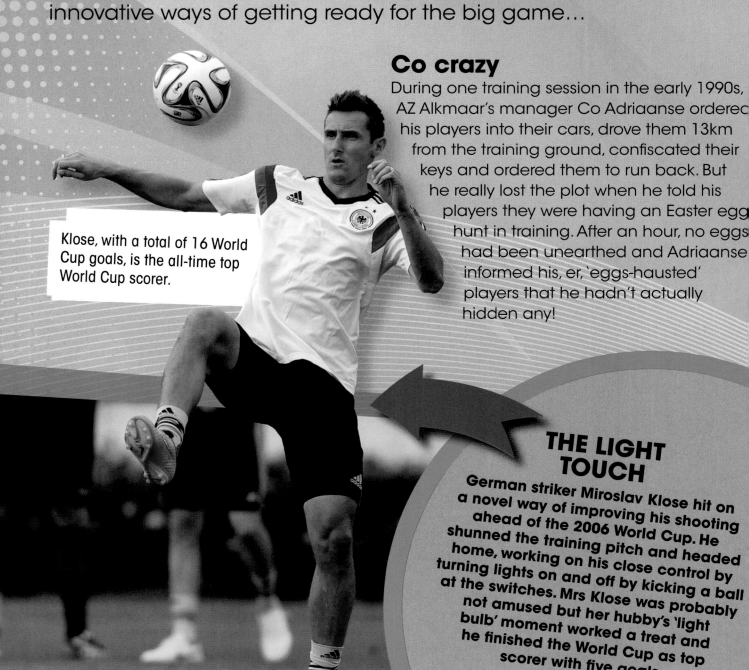

Most football folk believe a training session is all about fitness and practice, but the more forward-thinking managers and players have come up with far more innovative ways of getting ready for the big game…

Co crazy

During one training session in the early 1990s, AZ Alkmaar's manager Co Adriaanse ordered his players into their cars, drove them 13km from the training ground, confiscated their keys and ordered them to run back. But he really lost the plot when he told his players they were having an Easter egg hunt in training. After an hour, no eggs had been unearthed and Adriaanse informed his, er, 'eggs-hausted' players that he hadn't actually hidden any!

Klose, with a total of 16 World Cup goals, is the all-time top World Cup scorer.

THE LIGHT TOUCH

German striker Miroslav Klose hit on a novel way of improving his shooting ahead of the 2006 World Cup. He shunned the training pitch and headed home, working on his close control by turning lights on and off by kicking a ball at the switches. Mrs Klose was probably not amused but her hubby's 'light bulb' moment worked a treat and he finished the World Cup as top scorer with five goals.

The tutu technique

Ballet and football are not natural bedfellows but the two did reluctantly join forces in 2003 when Queens Park Rangers headed off to the English National Ballet to get some unlikely tips on flexibility and stamina from the dancers. Disappointingly, the embarrassed QPR players refused to don the tutus on offer but after a few pirouettes, they headed back to Loftus Road to insist on long-distance runs only in future.

OUCH!

German manager Christoph Daum always enjoyed a reputation as an unconventional coach and during his four-year stint at Bayer Leverkusen in the late 1990s, he once ran over a pile of broken glass in bare feet to prove to his players the power of mind over matter. His squad politely declined to take their boots off, as Daum probably went to find the club doctor.

We don't know what he's cheering for – probably one of his players hurting himself!

TOUCHLINE CATWALK

All eyes are usually on the 22 men running around in shorts chasing the ball, but some managers don't like to feel left out. Whether they mean it or not, what they are wearing often becomes more interesting than the match itself…

Scarf mania

Trendsetting Italian Roberto Mancini looked so good in his 1950s-style Manchester City scarf that during Christmas 2009, the club shop was unable to keep up with the demand from fans desperate to recreate his suave look. The City boss even had the club's bigwigs copying him, by sporting the same style in the directors' box.

Here's Jogi wearing one of his trademark jumpers. Pose for the camera!

JOGI BLUE

German fans were simply obsessed by their national team coach Joachim Löw during the 2010 World Cup, but it was his fashion sense and not tactics that got the nation talking. Sporting a rather fetching v-neck sweater for each game, Löw gained many admirers and even 'created' a new shade of colour in the process. Sales of 'Jogi Blue' jumpers went through the roof to such an extent that Germans were even popping over to the Netherlands to pick up the summer's must-have garment.

Olsen was ready to help the groundsman put the divots back at half-time.

Sleeping bag

Every winter the usually dapper Arsenal manager Arsène Wenger lets himself down by donning a three-quarter-length puffa jacket that's big enough to keep half of the Gunners squad warm. Oversized and with no shape to it whatsoever, it has quite rightfully been compared to a sleeping bag!

Wenger is all wrapped up and ready to take a nap if the game gets a bit dull.

BOOT-IFUL BOSS

Norwegian manager Egil Olsen made a big impression when he became Wimbledon boss in 1999, not least because of his love of wellington boots. Eccentric Egil hated driving and could be seen walking to training in scruffy wellies and he often chose to wear the unusual footwear during matches too. The boots were such a hit that the club shop even began selling Olsen Wellies before he was sacked less than a year later.

CHAPTER 6
FANTASTIC FANS

Most supporters are happy to have their fun in the stands, whether it's with flamboyant fancy dress, daring dancing or funny flags. Of course, not all fans are always on their best behaviour – sometimes they can't resist a cheeky pitch invasion or finding another way of getting closer to the action than they should.

FOUR-TIME CHAMPS

After winning the World Cup in Brazil in 2014, a triumphant German team returned home for a massive victory celebration in their country's capital, Berlin. This was the fourth time Germany had won the competition, and around 500,000 deliriously happy fans turned out at the Brandenburg Gate to honour their heroes, who beat Argentina 1-0 in the final to claim the trophy.

KEEP OFF THE GRASS

The pitch is meant to only be for the 22 players, the match officials, managers in their technical areas and mascots desperate to be famous. However, the hallowed turf is sometimes forced to welcome some uninvited guests…

KUNG-FU KEEPER

Tough stewards and quick-thinking policemen are usually the ones that foil an adventurous pitch invader, but the Dutch Cup clash between Ajax and AZ Alkmaar in 2011 proved that angry goalies can be equally capable. Alkmaar keeper Esteban Alvarado took exception to a foray onto the pitch by an Ajax fan, flooring him with a flying kung-fu kick – and receiving a red card for his efforts.

Afterwards Alvarado said to the fan, "You could have at least pulled your trousers up, mate!"

Karl Power, here on the left, having his moment of fame before security noticed.

Not-so-super Mario waves to the crowd. That bandaged knee is fooling nobody!

Power prank

In 2001 the pre-match team photo presented Karl Power with the ideal opportunity to pull off one of the most daring pranks in football history when Manchester United faced Bayern Munich in the Champions League. Power got past security by pretending to be part of a TV crew and once he was pitchside at Old Trafford, he changed into his United kit and strolled out with the rest of the players for a photo. United defender Gary Neville soon rumbled him though!

WHEELY CHEEKY

The 2014 World Cup was notable for lots of exciting matches, and Belgium's Round of 16 clash with the USA was no exception. Early in the first half, however, play was interrupted by a gatecrasher in a Superman T-shirt. Mario Ferri had cheekily bagged himself a spot in the disabled section when, miracle-like, he leapt from his wheelchair and ran onto the pitch. Not so super…

DRESSED FOR THE OCCASION

Showing support for your team is usually limited to wearing a replica shirt or club scarf. But for some of the more flamboyant fans, especially when it comes to the big occasions, the more outrageous the match-day outfit the better.

GREEN AND ORANGE

It probably didn't take Republic of Ireland fans long to hit on the idea of dressing up as leprechauns during EURO 2012, but what their fancy dress lacked in originality, they more than made up for with effort. Over on the continent, fans of the Netherlands are known for dressing in their country's national colour of orange. There's even a name for it – 'oranjegekte', which means orange craze. So when it comes to the really big occasions, like the World Cup or European Championships, you can be sure to see some totally crazy orange outfits on display.

This Dutch big chief drums up support for his team as they take on Germany at EURO 2012.

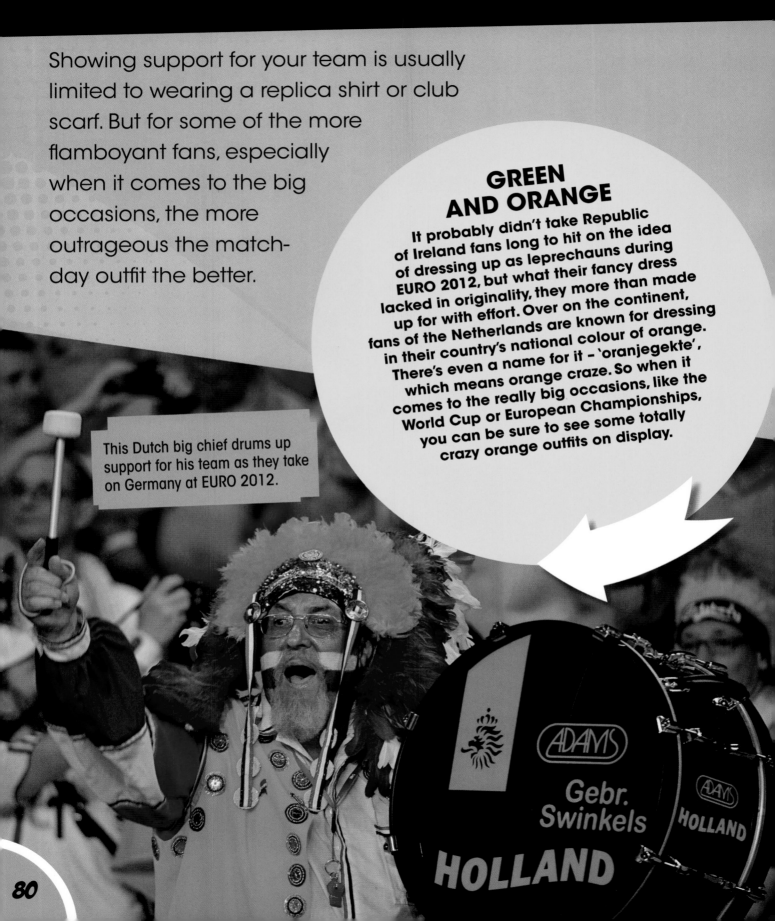

Rock 'n' roll Rodgers

When British bookmakers said that there was more chance of Elvis Presley being spotted alive than Swansea City avoiding relegation from the Premier League in 2011–12, the Welsh side not only proved them wrong, but comfortably survived the drop. And just to remind the bookies of their mistake, Swansea boss Brendan Rodgers called on the club's fans to come to the last home game of the season dressed as 'The King'. So of course, they did just that…

Why the Y-fronts?

While some fans prefer to dress up for the big match, supporters of Japanese Division One side Kashiwa Reysol decided to strip down to their underpants for their local derby with Kashiwa Antlers in 2000. Exactly why they got undressed has been lost in translation, but they certainly made an impression!

VIKING GIRL

This vocal Viking was seen in the crowd cheering Sweden on during their EURO 2012 clash with Ukraine in Kiev, proving once and for all that there isn't a fancy dress outfit that's too outrageous for a match. The costume also had an added benefit at half-time when the fan didn't like the look of the queue for the men's toilets.

Viking power couldn't stop the Swedes crashing to a 2-1 defeat to Ukraine.

Reporters often refer to great goals 'lighting up' a game but some supporters like to light things up in a different way, by ignoring the fireworks code and throwing flares all over the place. This can be very dangerous if they set fire to the flags they've also smuggled in.

Beside the seaside

Real Madrid fans opted for a nautical theme for the massive flag they unveiled at the Bernabeu at the end of the 2006–07 season before a clash with Real Mallorca. Luckily for the loyal home supporters, their title dreams didn't sink without a trace as Real pipped bitter rivals Barcelona to the title.

GRASS BURNS

Groundsmen spend hours and hours lovingly grooming their grass, so it's a safe bet the man in charge of the turf at the San Siro was less than impressed as fans littered his beautiful pitch with flares during a Milan derby in 2005. Inter's Juan Veron (far left) and Marco Materazzi look on in shock and amazement alongside AC Milan's Rui Costa.

Pride of Penarol

No football banner has ever come bigger or better than the whopping 1,500m², two-tonne yellow and black beauty made by fans of Uruguayan giants Penarol in 2011. The flag took four months to make and the fans raised £25,000 for all the material they needed. Carried to the stadium by 300 volunteers, when the flag was unfurled at a Copa Libertadores clash against Independiente, it stretched almost halfway around the entire stadium.

"Maybe if we stare at it for long enough, the smoke will go away."

Serbia's Stefan Mitrović grabs hold of the Albanian flag. All hell broke out just after this.

DRONING ON

When Serbia met Albania in a EURO 2016 qualifier in 2014, UEFA had anticipated the potential for trouble (the two countries have a troubled political history), and Albanian fans had been banned from travelling to Belgrade. The game had been fairly uneventful as half-time approached, but then things got rather heated. A remote-controlled drone appeared over the Serbian half with an Albanian flag attached to it. When it was grabbed by the Serbian players, the Albanians took exception and it descended into madness, eventually leading to the game being abandoned.

CHAPTER 7
AND FINALLY...

COLD COMFORT

It's an annual tradition for local residents in Shenyang in China to go for a swim in a frozen river at Christmas time, but before taking their dip, the hardy souls like to warm up with a quick kick-about on the ice. It must be great for sliding tackles...

This is the section for the crazy football stories that don't fit into any other – from ancient traditions that take us away from the millionaire players and high-tech stadiums, and back to the origins of football, to what goes on in the outer fringes of the game. So let's sign off with some obsessive record breakers and find out about some footballers' misadventures with music.

The professional game may boast the glitz and the glamour (and of course, money) but that's not to say village football doesn't produce its fair share of drama and funny stories, proving that bigger doesn't always mean better.

In Bungay versus Bungay, the players ranged in age from 4 to 68!

WHAT'S IN A NAME?

In one game in 2012 at Bungay FC in Suffolk, England, all 22 players, the referee, linesmen, substitutes and even the mascots were called Bungay. The idea for the bizarre game came from club official Shaun Cole, who invited Bungays from Britain, the USA and Australia to take part in the match for charity. "I thought the idea for the match was nuts when it was first suggested and it's still nuts today," Cole said.

The World Player of the Year…
Lionelly-the-elephant Messi!

And the final score was…
tree-nil!

GIANT'S GAME

According to legend, elephants never forget but these supersized players clearly didn't remember their shin pads at the Surin Elephant Round-Up Festival in Thailand, an annual opportunity for the big beasts to show-off their soccer skills. Standing on the ball is discouraged, while it's an automatic red card for any elephant sneakily attempting to trip an opponent with its trunk.

Tree hazard

The sunshine in Brazil can be seriously energy-sapping, but back in the 1990s any team playing on this pitch in a rural region of the country could find some very welcome shade under a handily placed tree. It must have proved an unusual obstacle, especially for visiting sides who weren't accustomed to playing with a tree on the pitch…

BACK TO MY ROOTS

The game as we know it has been entertaining fans for around 150 years but the history of the sport goes back much, much further – as these weird and wonderful examples of early versions of football prove...

Sales of replica kemari kits took a dive when this multi-coloured number was introduced.

AERIAL BOMBARDMENT

Basically an early Japanese version of keepie-uppie, 'kemari' is nearly 1,500 years old and involves a team of players repeatedly heading, kicking and even elbowing a small sphere in a desperate bid to stop it hitting the floor. The ball, called a mari, was traditionally made from deerskin and was possibly the inspiration for the modern hacky sack.

Super soule

La soule is a mad mash-up of football, rugby and hockey dating from medieval times that was played in parts of northern France. Teams from two villages would aim to get the 'ball' (usually a pig's bladder or a leather sack stuffed with straw) back to a certain place using hands, feet or sticks. The teams battled across fields, woods and through ditches and ponds. It is played today, sometimes in historic dress and traditionally on or around Shrove Tuesday. Similar games are played in England and Belgium, too.

The ancient game of La soule, shown here in a special stamp from Monaco.

CALCIO KICKS

Created in the Italian city of Florence over 500 years ago, 'Calcio Fiorentino' ('Florentine kick game') is still played today and if you've got a giant sand pit, 54 players (27 per team) and eight officials, you could have a match. Players can use feet and hands, and goals are scored by throwing the ball over a marked spot on the edge of the square pitch. Head-butting, choking and punching are all legal but they draw the line at kicks to the head!

Foot up

Football's answer to volleyball, 'sepak takraw' is a popular game in Malaysia and Thailand that dates back 600 years and although you'll need a net to play, there are no goalies. Two teams of three players line up on a pitch about the size of a badminton court and kick, volley and head a small ball over a 1.5-metre net. With points and sets, the scoring system is similar to tennis.

However the player from the blue team goes in, he's not going to get the ball!

Most coaches encourage their players to keep the ball on the ground, but as these mind-blowing examples prove, some people are simply born to keep the football in the air.

Head case

Balancing the ball on your head is a tricky talent that most of us find impossible, but Nigeria's Harrison Chinedu has practised the technique to perfection. In 2016 he set a new world record for walking while balancing a football atop his head, covering 48.04km along the Lagos Express road to the National Stadium.

Coordinated capers

The Linzi District of China claims (among many other places) to be the birthplace of football, and it was there, in 2011, that 1,377 school students set a new world record for the most people doing keepie-uppie at the same time. They broke the previous record of 1,062, also set in China, two years previously.

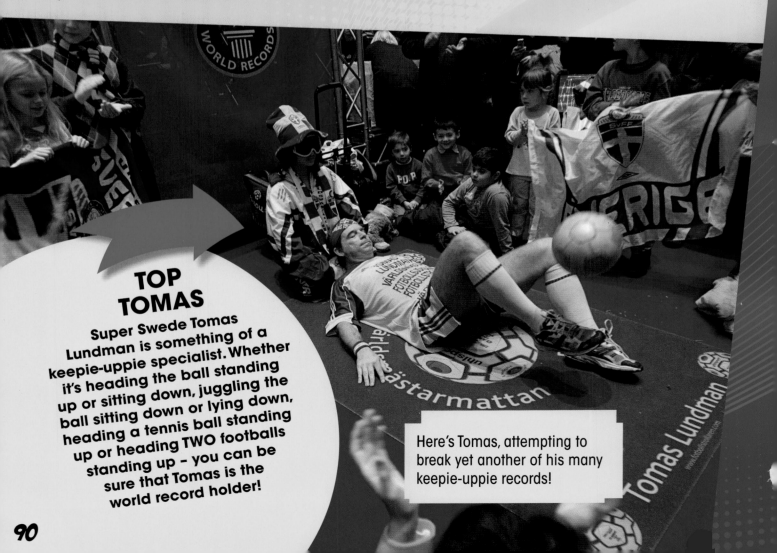

TOP TOMAS

Super Swede Tomas Lundman is something of a keepie-uppie specialist. Whether it's heading the ball standing up or sitting down, juggling the ball sitting down or lying down, heading a tennis ball standing up or heading TWO footballs standing up – you can be sure that Tomas is the world record holder!

Here's Tomas, attempting to break yet another of his many keepie-uppie records!

Tomas Lundman

Marathon man

The 42km of a marathon are the ultimate test of athletic endurance, but in 2011 England's John Farnworth decided to make the London race even more challenging, by foot-juggling a ball for the entire distance. Farnworth completed his crazy keepie-uppie mission by finishing the race in an impressive 12 hours and 15 minutes!

Farnworth can even do keepie-uppie in a smart suit!

MAGNESS MADNESS

Professional football freestyler Dan Magness could claim to be king of keepie-uppie. Not only did he set the record in 2010 for the longest time keeping the ball airborne (26 hours), but in the same year the incredible Englishman walked an unbelievable 58km of the streets of London without once letting the ball hit the pavement. He even visited all five of that season's Premier League grounds in London while he did it!

Here's Dan doing his thing outside Fulham's Craven Cottage ground.

Footballers' attempts at singing are usually limited to karaoke at the club Christmas party but unfortunately for us, some misguided players become convinced their talents deserve a wider audience and insist on actually releasing records.

Waddle and Hoddle

Chris Waddle reached number 20 in the UK charts in 1987 when he released the infamous 'Diamond Lights' with Spurs team-mate Glenn Hoddle, but the warbling winger had a second stab at pop stardom in France after he signed for Marseille in 1989, recording 'We've Got a Feeling' with team-mate Basil Boli. The video for the song featured cartoon zebras and the British Houses of Parliament.

Morten takes a break from his musical career to fit in a game for Blackburn.

MUSICAL MORTEN

With his bleached-blonde hair and youthful good looks, Norwegian midfielder Morten Ganst Pedersen always looked like a member of a boy band and after years of jokes about his 'look' he called everyone's bluff... by actually joining a boy band. Teaming up with professionals from the Norwegian Premier League, Pedersen became part of a group called The Players (they must have spent ages thinking of that name) and released a track called 'This is for Real'. Incredibly, the song was a big hit across Scandinavia.

Some of Kevin's team's fixtures had to be moved to avoid clashing with his appearances on Pop Idol!

FOOTBALL IDOL

Footballers' experiments with the music biz are rarely successful, but Kevin Walker seems to be the exception. In Sweden he turns out for top-flight side Djurgardens, but after injury put him out for a spell, he entered the Swedish version of Pop Idol in 2013 – and won!

I can't dance

These days Dutch legend Ruud Gullit sports a sensible short haircut, but in his playing days he was famous for his dreadlocks, so it was probably inevitable his first foray into music would be with a reggae track. Gullit's tune 'Not the Dancing Kind' was a small hit in 1984.

Cruyff's cringe

Dutch legend Johan Cruyff was famous for the legendary 'turn' he invented and which is still named after him. He's not famous, however, for his singing career which began (and ended) in 1969. If you're ever unlucky enough to hear his single – 'Oei Oei Oei (Dat Was Me Weer een Loei)' – you'll know exactly why. The oom-pah-style song is truly terrible and if you listen very carefully, you can almost hear Cruyff cringing with embarrassment as the band plays on.

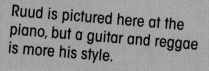

Ruud is pictured here at the piano, but a guitar and reggae is more his style.

Every footballer dreams of winning a trophy, and once the silverware has been lifted and the fans have gone home singing, the party can really start. Unfortunately though, the celebrations do not always go according to plan…

GOALKEEPER GAFFE

Netherlands goalkeeper Maarten Stekelenburg had a superb 2010–11 season as Ajax were crowned Dutch champions, but his normally safe hands spectacularly deserted him on an open-top bus ride through Amsterdam, dropping the trophy as he tried to pass it to team-mate Jan Vertonghen. An eagle-eyed policeman picked up the silverware before it was squashed by traffic and handed it to an eager Ajax supporter, who raced after the bus on foot in a desperate but hilarious effort to return the trophy.

Stekelenburg has a firm grip on the trophy here, unlike later on…

Torres looks at home, playing with the kids, after Spain's famous victory.

IN THE NIGHT GARDEN

Winning trophies is child's play for Fernando Torres. He starred in Spain's EURO 2008 final victory over Germany, scoring the only goal, then lifted the World Cup in 2010. After winning the FA Cup and Champions League with Chelsea in May 2012, Fernando scored in the EURO 2012 final against Italy. And he got a special prize for winning the Golden Boot: the right to look after his team-mates' children as they played in the post-match confetti.

Butter fingers

Real Madrid's Sergio Ramos proved players are definitely better with their feet than hands when he spectacularly dropped the Copa del Rey in 2011. Madrid were parading the cup on an open-top bus after beating Barcelona in the final when Ramos lifted it onto his head but let it slip through his fingers. The precious silverware went crashing down onto the road and underneath the wheels of the bus!

Karate crazy

Kicks to the head are an occupational hazard in football, but players don't expect to get a battering after the final whistle. That's what happened to Antonio Cassano in 2011 after AC Milan won the Italian title. Cassano was giving a post-match interview when team-mate Zlatan Ibrahimović karate-kicked the side of his face. Whether the pair kissed and made up as the party in the dressing room got into full swing remains a mystery...

The publishers would like to thank the following sources for their kind permission to reproduce the pictures in this book.

Action Images: Reuters: 36 (bottom), 84-85; /Lee Smith: 62 (bottom)

Getty Images: AFP: 61; /Keiny Andrade/LatinContent: 59; /Mladen Antonov/AFP: 5 (top left), 55 (centre); /The Asahi Shimbun: 79 (bottom); /L.Baron: 66-67; /Alexandre Battibugli: 87 (centre); /James Baylis/AMA; /Peter Bischoff: 63 (top); /Jimmy Bolcina/Photonews: 37; /Lionel Bonaventure/AFP: 55 (right); /Bongarts: 16; /Shaun Botterill/Allsport: 79 (top); /Gabriel Bouys/AFP: 9 (bottom); /Phil Cole/Allsport: 12; /Vinicius Costa: 44 (bottom); /Adrian Dennis/AFP: 72; /Hoang Dinh Nam/AFP: 18-19; / Denis Doyle: 38; /Emmanuel Dunand/AFP: 5 (bottom), 52-53; /Paul Ellis/AFP: 10-11, 51, 65 (top); /Bertil Enevåa Ericson/TT/AFP: 93 (top); /Francisco Estrada/Jam Media/LatinContent: 28; /Paul Gilham: 16-17, 74; /Tristan Fewings: 90 (top); /Laurence Griffiths: 24, 45, 95; /Sergei Grits/AP: 81; /Valery Hache/AFP: 46; /Alexander Hassenstein/Bongarts: 60-61; /Patrick Hertzog/AFP: 22 (centre); /Mike Hewitt: 1, 53, 82-83; /Hulton Archive: 44 (centre); /Andrej Isakovic/AFP: 83 (top); /Toussaint Kluiters/AFP: 94; /Christof Koepsel/Bongarts: 19 (right); /Uwe Kraft/ullstein bild: 73 (bottom); /Xavier Laine: 34-35; /Bryn Lennon: 32 (bottom), 81 (top); /Matthew Lewis: 62 (top), 92; /Alex Livesey: 13, 49 (top), 68; /John Macdougall/AFP: 25; / Stuart MacFarlane: 75 (left); /Robert Michael/AFP: 76-77; /Jonathan Nackstrand: 26-27; /Thomas Niedermueller/Bongarts: 11 (bottom); /Kazuhiro Nogi/AFP: 88 (centre); /John Peters/Man Utd: 11 (top); /Joern Pollex/Bongarts: 21; /Popperfoto: 32 (top), 34 (left); /Mike Powell: 48-49; /Savo Prelevic/AFP: 15; /Gary Prior: 75 (right); /Michael Regan: 5 (top right), 69 (right); /Martin Rose/Bongarts: 50-51; /STR/AFP: 39; /Jewel Samad/AFP: 40-41; /Genya Savilov/AFP: 80; /Lefty Shivambu/Gallo Images: 58; /Ben Stansall/AFP: 91 (bottom); /Dave Stamboulis: 87 (top); /Thomas Starke/Bongarts: 65 (bottom); /Michael Steele: 47; /Boris Streubel: 6-7; /Bob Thomas: 19 (top), 34 (centre), 48 (bottom left), 69 (left); /Eric Vandeville/Gamma-Rapho: 89; /VI Images: 78; /Hiroki Watanabe: 36 (top); /Andrew Yates/AFP: 14 (bottom)

Mirrorpix: 20 (top & bottom)

Offside Sports Photography: 31 (top)

Press Association Images: AP Photo/Keystone/Marcel Bieri: 2, 64; /Mike Egerton/Empics Sport: 70; /Empics Sport: 22 (bottom); /Nigel French/Empics Sport: 71; /Martin Meissner/AP: 52 (centre); /Henrik Montgomery/TT/TT News Agency: 90; /Nils Petter Nilsson/XP/Scanpix/TT News Agency: 8 (top); /Nick Potts: 29; /Sydsvenkan/Scanpix/TT News Agency: 31 (bottom); /Anders Wiklund/AP: 54

Private Collection: 32-33, 60

REX/Shutterstock: 5 (top centre), 30, 93 (bottom); /Albanpix Ltd: 86; /Colorsport: 14 (top); /James Marsh/BPI: 23

Shutterstock.com: 63 (bottom), 73 (top), 88 (bottom)

Every effort has been made to acknowledge correctly and contact the source and/or copyright holder of each picture and Carlton Books Limited apologises for any unintentional errors or omissions, which will be corrected in future editions of this book.